LITTLE INSECTS
Coloring Book

Winky Adam

DOVER PUBLICATIONS, INC.
Mineola, New York

Note

Insects of many shapes and sizes are found almost everywhere in the world. This book contains pictures of sixty of them, listed in alphabetical order, for you to color and study, along with coloring instructions. Because insects are often very small, many of the renderings are much larger than life.

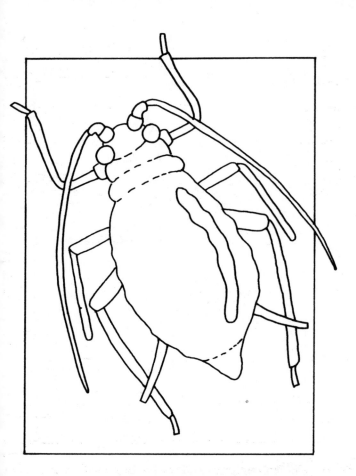

Aphid.   Variable coloring—often green.

1

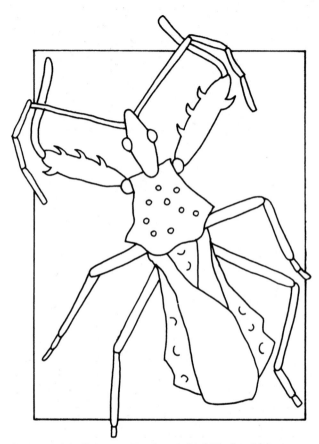

Assassin Bug. Red with blackish-brown markings.

2

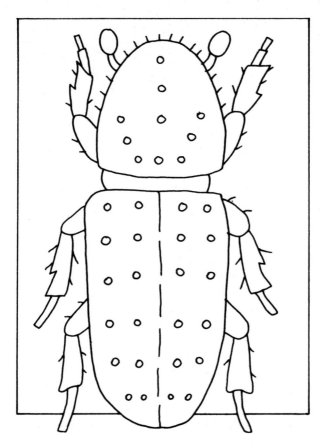

Bark Beetle. Shiny reddish-brown, dark brown or black.

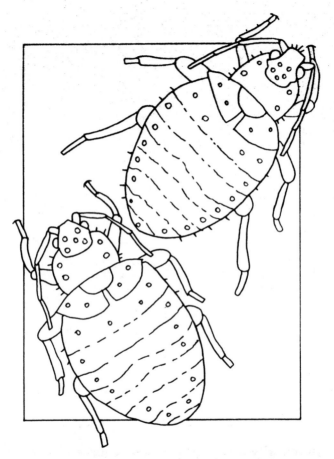

Bedbug. Rusty red to purplish.

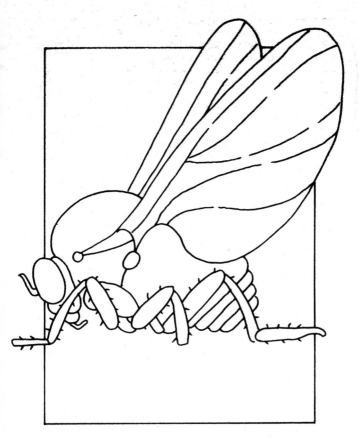

Black Fly. Grayish-brown to shiny black; clear wings.

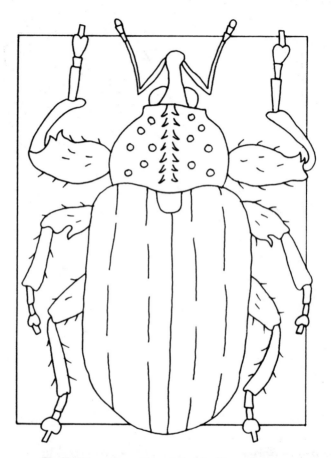

Boll Weevil. Grayish-black to brown.

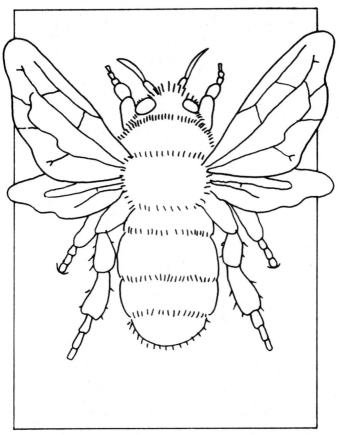

Bumblebee. Body has alternating black and yellow stripes, with smoky-gray wings.

7

Butterfly. Magnificently colored wings, differing with each species.

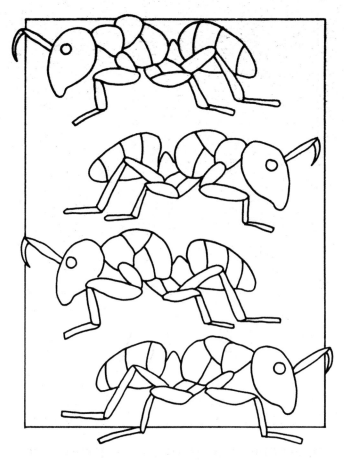

Carpenter Ant. Black or red.

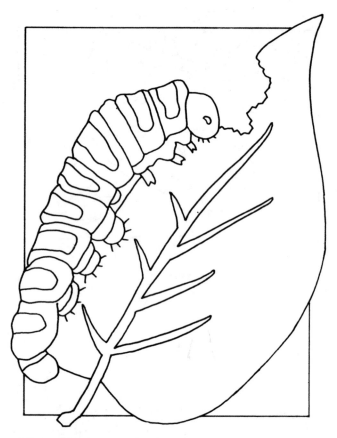

Caterpillar. Variable coloring. Caterpillars are the young of butterflies.

Cicada. Brown, black or greenish.

11

Click Beetle. Shiny dark gray with white markings.

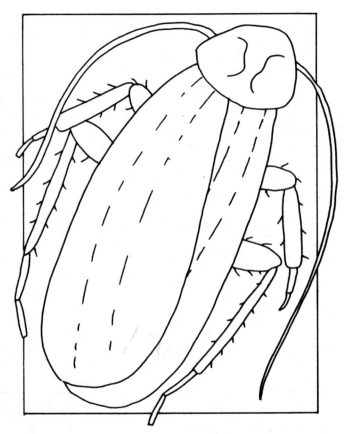

Cockroach. Dark to reddish-brown with yellowish markings.

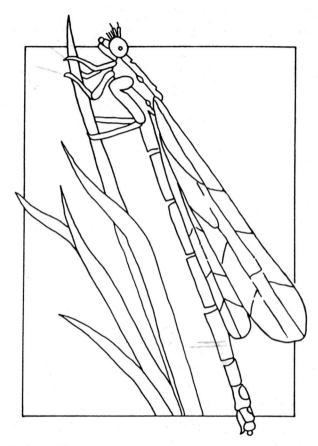

Damselfly. Can be many different colors—
most often blue or black.

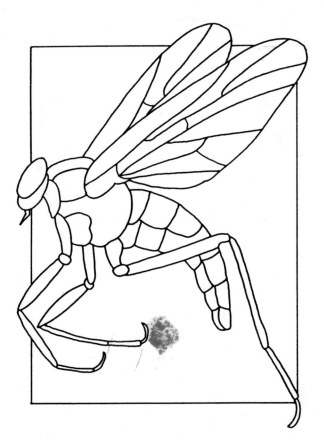

Deer Fly. Bright green or gold eyes; body black with yellow markings.

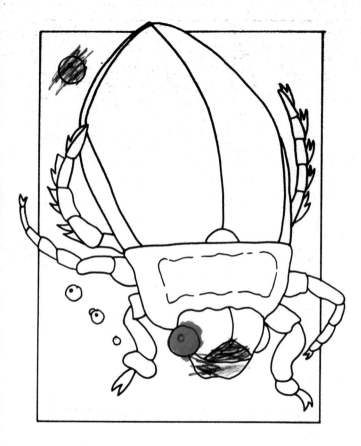

Diving Beetle. Brownish-black or dark green.

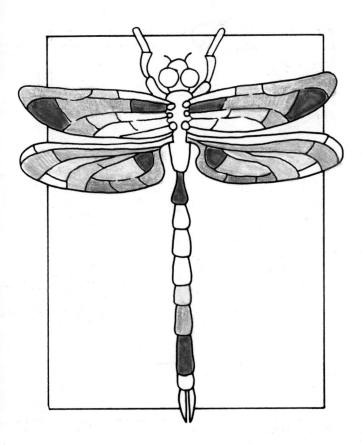

Dragonfly. Brilliant blue, green or black.

Dung Beetle. Dull black with bluish or greenish tinge.

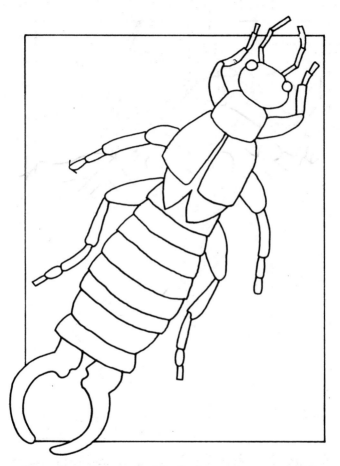

Earwig. Brown to black; long pincers at tail.

Field Cricket. Dark reddish-brown to black.

20

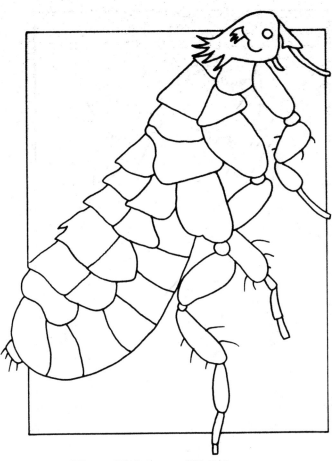

Flea. Pale- to reddish-brown.

21

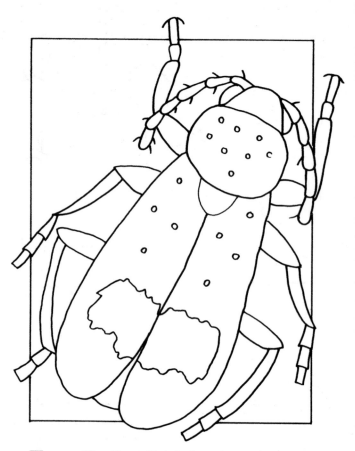

Flower Beetle. Brightly colored in metallic tints.

Frog Beetle. Black with a metallic red or green tint.

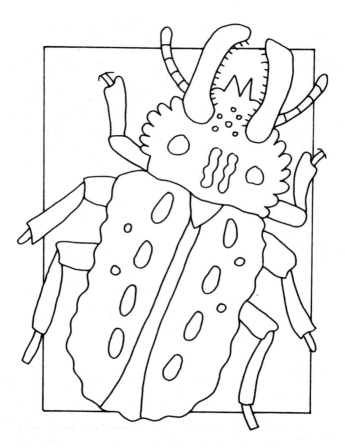

Fungus Beetle. Black with red, orange, yellow or purple patterns.

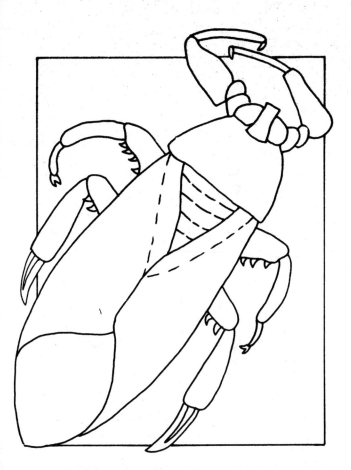

Giant Water Bug. Brown.

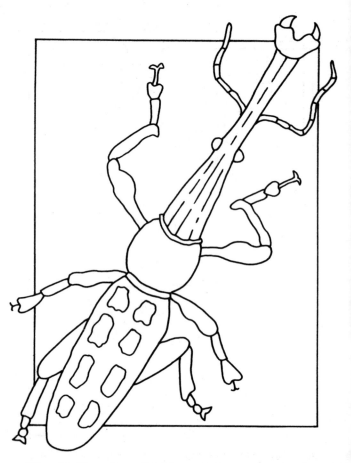

Giraffe Beetle.   Black with brown markings.

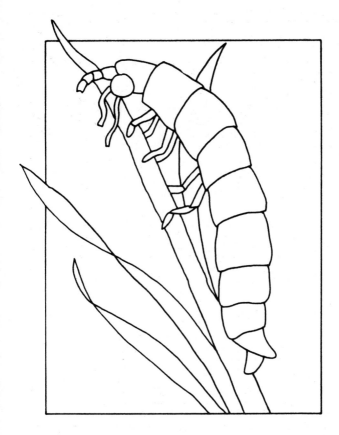

Glow-Worm. Whitish. It is the larva, or first stage, of a lightning bug.

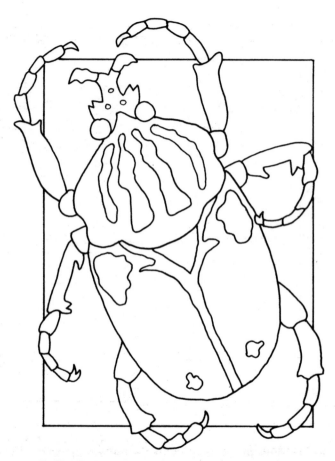

Goliath Beetle. Gray, white and black.

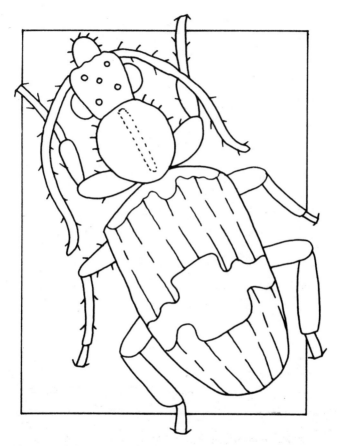

Ground Beetle. Shiny black; legs and antennae reddish-brown.

Gypsy Moth. Yellowish-white with brown lines along edges of wings.

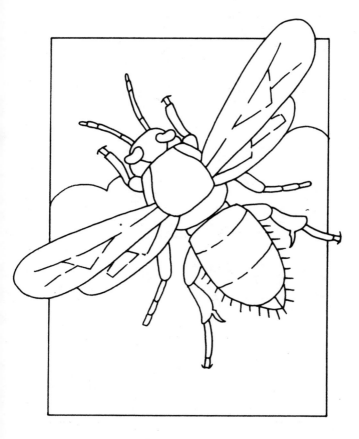

Hornet. Dull brown or black, sometimes banded with white.

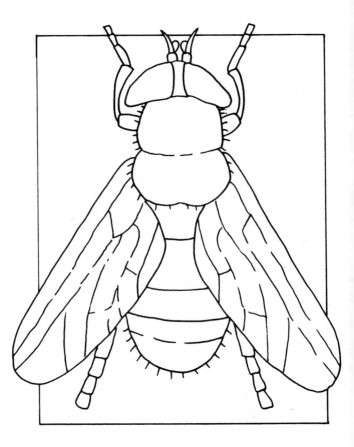

Horsefly. Eyes brownish-gray or metallic green, body black.

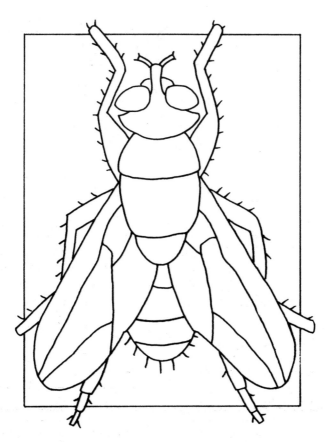

Housefly. Gray, with reddish eyes and clear wings.

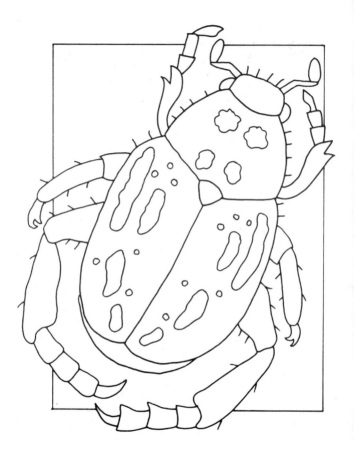

Japanese Beetle. Metallic green with brownish-orange wing covers.

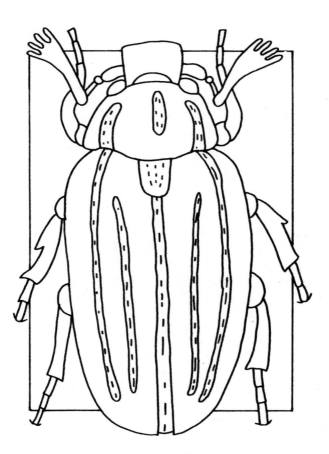

June Bug. Its hard, shell-like body is brown or black.

Lacewing. Clear wings, green or brown bodies, and long dangling legs.

Ladybug.   Red, orange or yellow with black markings, varied number of spots.

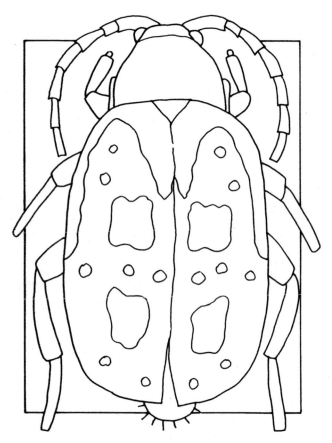

Leaf Beetle. Yellowish with black or brown markings.

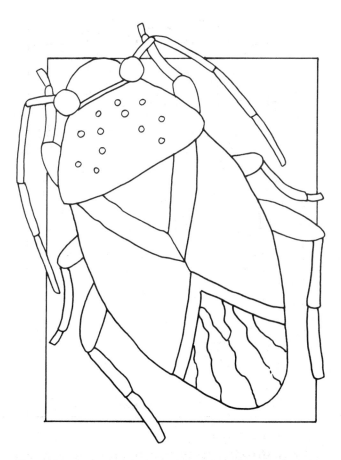

Leaf Bug. Brightly colored in various hues.

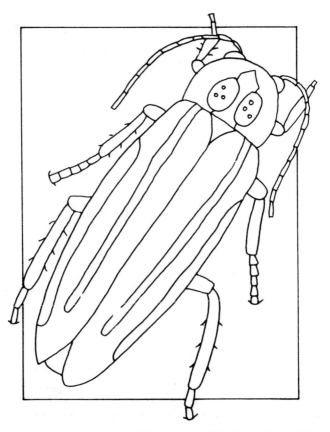

Lightning Bug. Brown or black body with red markings along wings; blinking green or yellow tail.

Locust. Brown, tan or green, matching its habitat.

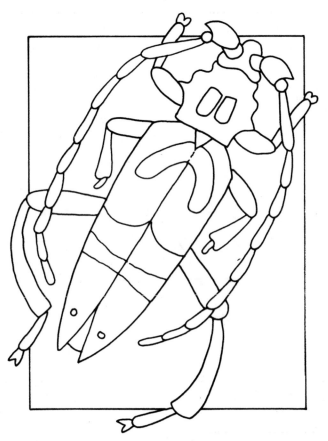

Long-Horned Beetle. Black with yellow markings.

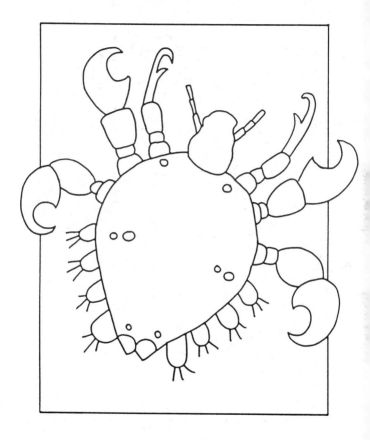

Louse. Gray or reddish-brown.

Luna Moth. Pale green wings and body; front wings are edged with purple.

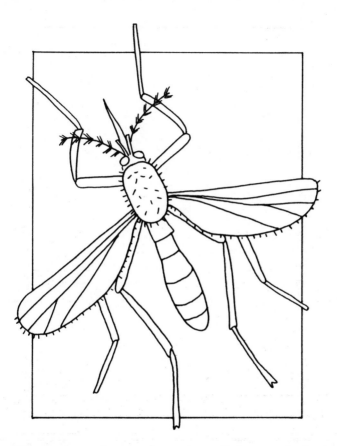

Mosquito. Long, sharp "nose"; brown body and wings.

Praying Mantis. Green to tan, with tan to brown eyes.

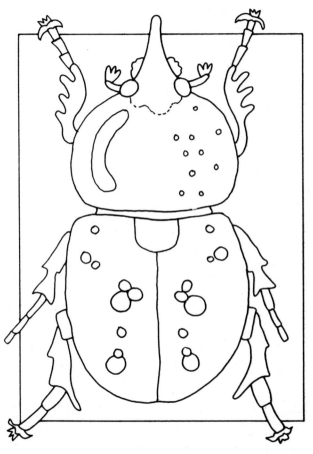

Rhinoceros Beetle.   Shiny black shell.

47

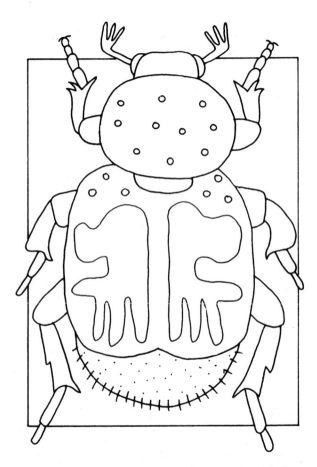

Scarab Beetle. Beautiful metallic colors.

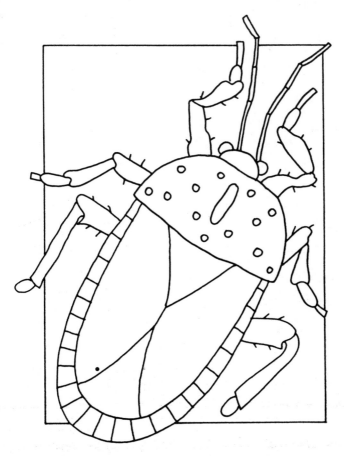

Shield Bug.   Found in many bright colors.

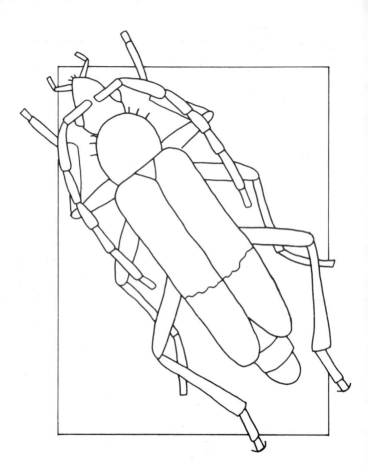

Soldier Beetle. Brownish-yellow or black.

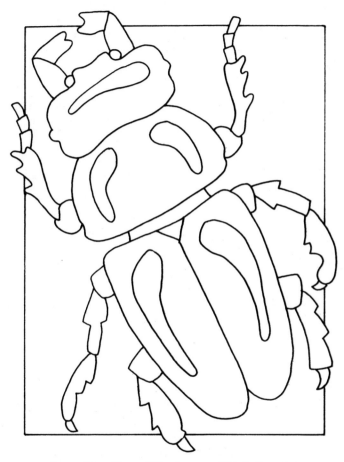

Stag Beetle. Black or reddish-brown.

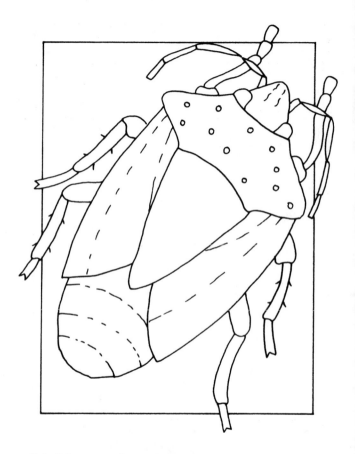

Stinkbug. Usually bright green with a stripe of yellow, orange or red at the edges.

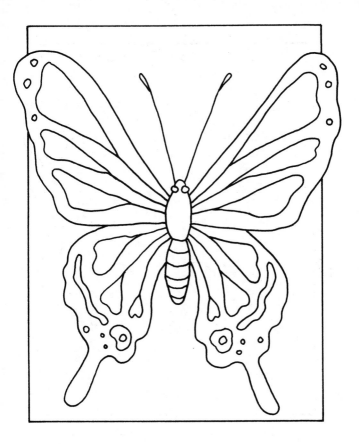

Swallowtail Butterfly. Black, yellow or white with red or blue spots.

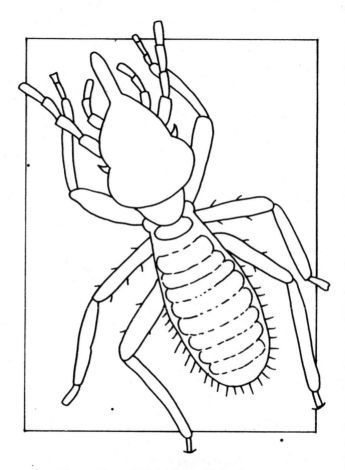

Termite. Whitish to light brown.

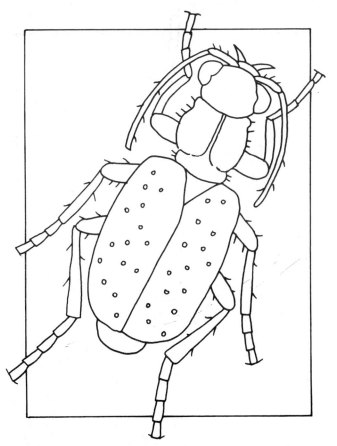

Tiger Beetle. Bronze, blue, green, purple or orange, with black markings.

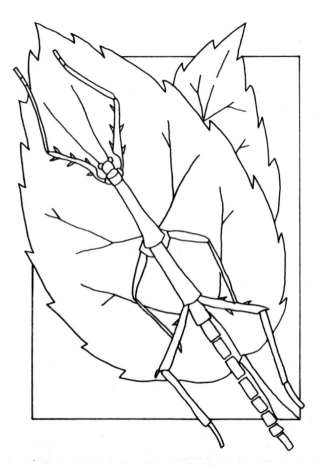

Walkingstick.   Light brown or green.

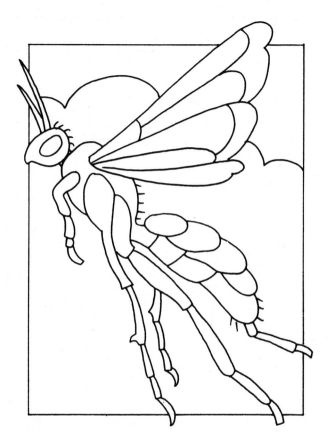

Wasp. Dull brown or black, with a noticeably thin "waist."

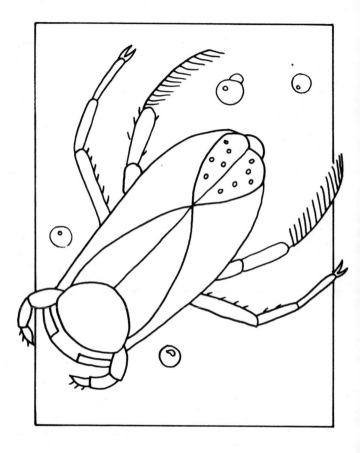

Water Boatman. Gray to brown.

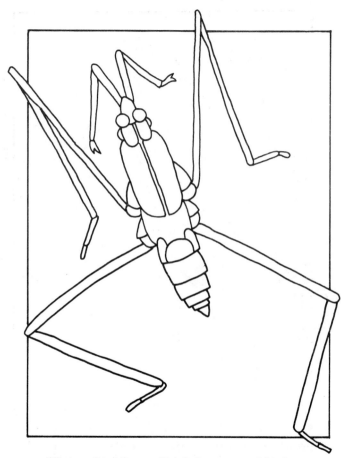

Water Strider. Dark brown to black.

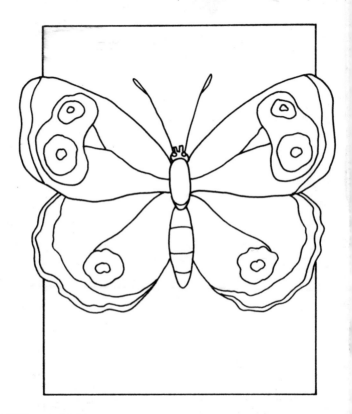

Wood Nymph Butterfly. Wings chocolate brown with yellow patches, containing blue eye-spots edged with black.

60